BEGINN

Christian Views of the Early Embryo

by

A Caroline Berry

Consultant Clinical Geneticist,
Guy's Hospital, London

Published by
CHRISTIAN MEDICAL FELLOWSHIP
LONDON

First published 1993

Christian Medical Fellowship
157 Waterloo Road
London SE1 8XN

ISBN 0-906747-27-9

Printed in Great Britain by
Stanley L Hunt (Printers) Ltd, Midland Road, Rushden, Northamptonshire

CONTENTS

ACKNOWLEDGEMENTS

The author wishes to thank:

Elizabeth Manners for her word-processing skills; and Alan Johnston and Julia Marsden for helpful comments on the text.

Some of the ideas expressed here originally appeared in the author's *Rites of Life,* published by Hodder and Stoughton in 1987 but now out of print.

Chapter I
Introduction

Identifying one's friends from photographs taken in infancy or childhood always makes a good ice-breaker at a party. We see nuances - sometimes much more than nuances - of the person we now know, and yet they look so different: their size, their clothes, their vulnerability. So different, and yet the same, with continuity stretching over the decades. Similar amazement arises at any 25-year anniversary or reunion. We meet one-time familiar fellow-travellers with whom we shared the traumas of tutorials and Finals. Some look unchanged, others very different, but the underlying people are still the same, often recognizable more by their gestures and mannerisms of speech than their outward appearance. There are some changes for better, some for worse, but their distinctiveness remains. We accept that there is continuity of the essential person, despite the changing appearance of the body they inhabit. The science of Embryology takes us further into our past. It tells us how our physical bodies are formed, and that we are wonderfully made. Lewis Wolpert, Professor of Anatomy at University College London, who has spent his life studying the embryo, states 'No one who studies development can fail to be filled with a sense of wonder and delight'.[1]

Embryological investigation does not, however, tell us about the person within the body. Two human cells, of limited value in themselves, fuse together, and nine months later a baby lies in a crib. We started with no person; we end with a new member of the human family.

When the infant received this imprint of personhood has been debated for centuries. Some philosophers base their understanding of personhood on physical attributes that distinguish humans from animals. They argue that even the new-born baby is not yet a true person in that (s)he has no capacity to reason or to respond in a distinctly human manner.[2] If full membership of the human family depends on our intellectual attributes, then this is a reasonable assessment of the infant, but it would also exclude those born with mental handicap, and those who develop dementia. For those accepting Judaeo-Christian teaching, with its emphasis on the value of the weak and the vulnerable, such a view is untenable. We must acknowledge that the newborn in the cot, or, for that matter, the very low birthweight 'prem' in the incubator, are small people in their own right, and deserving of care and protection (see *Survival of the Weakest*[3]).

We agree that newborns should be cherished, but we may disagree on the stage in development at which such value is attributed. Many Christians believe that from the moment of fertilization a person is present, and the fertilized ovum therefore of inestimable value. Other Christians find this an impossible position. As Christians, the view that matters to us is God's view, and it is the aim of this booklet to try to explore this. In the past, the only area of medicine to which the matter was relevant was the abortion issue. The topic has been long and intensely debated,[4,5] but Christian discussion has generally focused on the relative values of mother and fetus, and those Christians who accept abortion as permissible see it as a 'lesser evil'. Now, however, with the advent of *in vitro* fertilization techniques, the attributes and value of the fertilized ovum have become of importance, and Christians need to discover how the embryo pre- and post-implantation fits into God's scheme.

How can we, as his creatures, possibly hope to understand the mind of God? We know his thoughts are higher than our thoughts, and his ways than our ways. Job cries out in despair 'His wisdom is profound, his power vast ... ' (Jb 9:4).

But, as Christians, we believe that God has graciously revealed himself, in the whole of Scripture but particularly in the person of Jesus and the accounts of his life among us. Although there is little direct teaching in the Bible on embryonic life, we do have general principles which we can apply to this and other difficult areas. We accept that God has instituted the marriage relationship, and that children are given as a gift, valuable in their own right but to be nurtured and taught within the security of the family. God also understands the heartbreak of infertility, and dealt graciously with a number of women distressed by this problem (Sarah, in Gn 18; Samson's mother, in Jdg 13; Hannah, in 1 Sa 1, and Elizabeth, in Lk 1:5-25). We believe, too, that God is concerned with the individual, and deals with each of us as individuals. The weak and the vulnerable are his special concern, and the vigorous are delegated to mediate his concern. Our difficulty is to know when the individual begins.

Jesus said 'I am the Way, *the Truth,* and the Life'. Paul puts the belt of truth first in his list of Christian armour (Eph 6:14). We must seek Truth, and not be afraid of exploring its many facets and their implications. Yet here we must be careful to keep our perspectives right. The debate on 'When does personhood begin?', though important, is not a fundamental part of Christian faith. It is a secondary issue, and not one of the foundations on which our faith should be based.

This is a relatively new area for Christians to explore. We need not be afraid of disagreement. In fact, it may be by disagreement and re-thinking that we can make progress in our understanding. We all approach both Scripture and our understanding of Christian truth with the 'baggage' of our upbringing and life experience, and these may sometimes shape our understanding. God's truth is so large that we may not grasp all its facets at once, certainly initially. We need, therefore, to be wise in our weighing-up of the issues, and pray, in words written hundreds of years ago by the medieval scholar Rupert Meldenius, that we may have:

Unity in essentials
Liberty in incidentals
In all things Charity

We start our search with the biology of early fetal development. God is our creator, and throughout history, his followers have seen his handiwork in the natural order, and we will endeavour to do the same as we study early embryonic development.

Chapter II
Biology

This section briefly traces development of the human embryo from fusion of sperm and ovum to the moment of birth, with specific focus on the implications of the different stages in relation to 'personhood'.

Our molecular beginning

Every sperm contains 23 chromosomes, each of which is one of a pair carrying between them half of their generator's complement of deoxyribonucleic acid (DNA). The egg, with its 23 chromosomes, does likewise, but its cytoplasm also includes mitochondria with their independent system of mitochondrial DNA. The DNA molecule is made up of two coiled and complementary strands, held together by the bonds between complementary base pairs. There are four bases: adenine, thymine, guanine and cytosine. The first always pairs with the second, and the third with the fourth of these. The double-stranded molecule replicates itself by separation of the two strands, and each strand acts as a template on which to build a new complementary strand. The varying sequences of the bases code for different amino acids, which can then be assembled to give the different proteins and enzymes of which living cells are made.

We now know much more about this genetic code, and that there are not only sequences which initiate amino acid synthesis, but others, perhaps more important, which provide information on when coding should stop and start, and which sequences should be omitted. One of the most fascinating aspects of DNA biology is that essentially the same sequence system operates in both plant and animal kingdoms, so that human DNA can readily be inserted into a virus, a bacterium, or any other organism. The sequences coding for many essential enzymes are amazingly similar in organisms as widely separated as yeast and humans, so that the finding of a 'conserved sequence' (ie one that is similar in a number of other species) is a useful clue to the research worker that this may be an important functional sequence.

After fusion, a fertilized ovum contains the full DNA complement of three thousand million base pairs. The new individual will eventually produce their own eggs or sperm, so passing their DNA to the next generation. It has been said that our children are simply a means by which our genes can reach the 21st and any following centuries. The genes we express today were present, for better or worse, in our parents, grandparents and into the dim recesses of our family tree.

The genetic message is continuous, but expresses itself differently in each individual, giving us the person we know. This is because during the process of meiosis the genetic information is shuffled through the intertwining of the chromosomes, with the result that each sperm and ovum is genetically unique, as will be the product of their fusion. Although 90% of human DNA appears to have no active function, we are still left with 30 million active base pairs which code for every inherent characteristic of the person represented there. Already parts of the human genome have been sequenced, and the order of the individual base pairs is established for the entirety of some of the smaller 'genes', such as that coding for Factor IX, whose deficiency gives rise to Haemophilia B. *(See Fig 1 on page 11.)*

Already the entire sequences of some primitive organisms such as particular viruses are known, as is probably 20% of that of the genetic researchers' favourite creature, the fruit fly *Drosophila*. It can only be a matter of time before the entire genome of more complex creatures, including humans, is sequenced. The Human Genome Project is an international co-operative effort aiming to achieve this end, and vast sums of money are being poured into it, of the order of 200 million dollars per year. If this continues, it is likely to achieve its object by the turn of the century, and we will then know the three thousand million combinations of the four bases (adenine, guanine, thymine and cytosine) which characterise the human make-up. Eventually, variations which lead to serious disease will be disentangled from variations which have trivial or no effects, and each individual could be known by his or her characteristic unique sequence.

Is this important? People argue about the use of so much money, and whether the likely benefits warrant the investment. Others are concerned that such research into the basic structure of human beings is too presumptuous. From the point of view of embryology, however, the important aspect is that the potential for knowing the sequence is already present, and that embryology, or the study of beginnings, can now start at the most basic 'viral' stage of our existence, when we are in effect simply a printout of our three thousand million base pairs. The Christian has to ask 'does this printout bear the image of God?' Is it my brother or sister for whom Christ died, or is it the 'dust of the earth', which became a living being only as God breathed into it when he formed humans (Gn 2:7)? Is it a precious creation, or simply a set of building materials awaiting assembly? If we impute too great a value to our molecular make-up, we find that the person becomes simply the sum of his/her genes. The capacity for faith and a propensity to sin are inherent in our humanity, but are not coded by our DNA. There is no prospect of gene manipulation giving us peace with God.

Figure 1

```
A T G C A G C G C G T G A A C A T G A T
C A T G G C A G A A T C A C C A G G C C
T C A T C A C C A T C T G C C T T T T A
G G A T A T C T A C T C A G T G C T G A
A T G T A C A G T T T T T C T T G A T C
A T G A A A A C G C C A A C A A A A T T
C T G A A T C G G C C A A A G A G G T A
T A A T T C A G G T A A A T T G G A A G
A G T T T G T T C A A G G G A A C C T T
G A G A G A G A A T G T A T G G A A G A
A A A G T G T A G T T T T G A A G A A G
C A C G A G A A G T T T T T G A A A A C
A C T G A A A G A A C A A C T G A A T T
T T G G A A G C A G T A T G T T G A T G
G A G A T C A G T G T G A G T C C A A T ...
```

The first 300 bases (A = adenine, G = guanine, C = cytosine, T = thymine) of the gene for the blood clotting Factor IX. Any error gives rise to Haemophilia B (Christmas Disease).

The full coding sequence has 2,770 bases, and if the non-coding 'introns' are included, the full length is 34,000 bases. A virus sequence would look similar, and have around 200,000 bases in total.

The printout for the total genetic code (3 thousand million bases) for any individual person would be similar to that of a thousand Bibles!

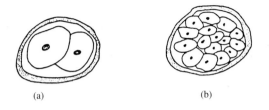

(a)   (b)

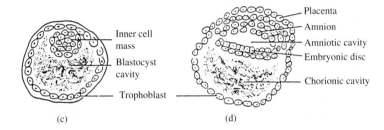

(c)   (d)

Figure 2   Early stages in the development of the embryo

(a) Two-celled stage, day 1;   (b) morula, day 4;
(c) blastocyst, day 6;   (d) early implantation, day 11

Reproduced by permission of Oxford University Press from *The Biology of Twinning in Man,*
Bulmer M G (1970)

Fertilization and onwards

We speak glibly of fertilization being the fusion of sperm and egg, but the process is a complicated one, with important mechanisms that allow a single sperm to penetrate the ovum, which then is able to repel the invasion of further sperms. Initially the fertilized ovum appears to function on its own genetic mechanism, and the sperm's genes are not expressed for some twenty-four hours or more. *(See Fig 2 on page 12.)*

For about ten days after fertilization, the fertilized ovum floats freely, first in the Fallopian tube, and then in the uterine cavity. This pre-implantation stage is an interesting one. Cell divisions occur which repeatedly double the number of cells present, so that the pre-implantation embryo can be characterised as four-cell, eight-cell, etc, and eventually as a morula, or solid ball of cells. During these early stages it is characterised by extreme plasticity. It can divide into two and give rise to genetically identical (monozygotic) twins. The cells are totipotent (ie each cell has the capacity to develop into any organ or other part of the body), so that one or two cells can be removed with impunity, and the remaining cells will continue to divide and develop undeterred. Work on *in vitro* fertilization shows that many of these pre-implantation embryos have lethal abnormalities, often numerical chromosomal errors, so that only about 50% of fertilized ova have the potential to succeed. There is thus a natural 'wastage' rate of about 50%.

Some conceptions effectively have no genetic contribution from the ovum, having 46 chromosomes coming from two sperm. Such a pregnancy may progress for some weeks, but will eventually form a hydatidiform mole. Other conceptions continue with three sets of chromosomes instead of the normal two, but will either miscarry, give rise to a different type of mole, or to a fetus with the lethal malformations of triploidy.

The next stage - implantation

The *morula,* now having around 30 - 60 cells, enters the uterine cavity and becomes a hollow, fluid-filled ball; it is now known as a *blastocyst. (See Fig 2.)* At this stage it starts to implant in the uterine wall. Its cells lose their totipotency and become committed to forming the various parts of the embryo and its supporting membranes and placenta. Cells can no longer be removed with impunity, and if twinning occurs the twins remain conjoined. The cavity of the blastocyst separates the outer cells which will form the support system from the cells which will form the embryo itself, the inner cell mass. Implantation involves invasion of the uterine wall by the outer cells of the blastocyst, which thus becomes anchored and attached to the mother. The process of implantation, which occurs over several days, initiates a maternal hormonal response (secretion of human chorionic gonadotrophin) which represses menstruation and signals to the mother that pregnancy has started. Before this she was quite unaware of what was happening within her. Some methods of contraception such as the use of a 'coil' (intra-uterine device) probably act by preventing implantation of the fertilized ovum.

Fertilization versus implantation

Prior to implantation there is totipotency, the possibility of two individuals arising from one zygote, and no maternal recognition. After implantation there are individual embryo(s) distinguished by their primitive streak (see below) from their support system, and maternal recognition, at least at the biological level. Thus implantation is a crucial stage, and some would say that conception should be considered to occur at the time of implantation rather than at fertilization, as it is only now that the new organism becomes related to its nurturing mother, and thus able to proceed with its development. It was these crucial changes, leading to the appearance of the primitive streak at around fourteen days, that persuaded the Warnock Committee[6] (*see page 33*) to set fourteen days as the limit up to which embryo research was to be permitted.

Further development

As implantation proceeds, the cells of the inner cell mass continue their development. A central core of cells (the embryonic disc - Fig 2) separates the amniotic cavity from the yolk sac, and it is now the central core on which attention is centred. Cells multiply and migrate in a highly organised manner to produce a linear appearance, the *primitive streak.*

With further multiplication and migration, the three cell layers ectoderm, endoderm and mesoderm are formed, and each of these will have its particular responsibilities for tissue and organ formation. How cell multiplication and movement rates are controlled is not known, but all must ultimately be in response to signals received from the genetic code. As the early pathways are so similar in a wide variety of creatures, it is likely that similar signals, using perhaps concentrations of chemicals, or the position of a neighbouring cell, are orchestrated to make either a mouse or a human, depending on the genetic information present.

Once the embryonic layers are distinguished, development proceeds apace. The notochord forms a scaffold for the developing nervous system, and by four weeks after fertilization the primitive brain and spinal cord are formed; by five weeks spinal cord reflexes start to occur. The circulatory system develops in parallel, with blood islands starting to become visible at the end of week 3. At the same time the tubes forming the heart appear, and by day 24 are starting to beat.

Eyes, ears and limbs develop during the fifth and sixth weeks, and limb movements are visible on ultrasound by seven weeks. By 10 - 11 weeks post-fertilization organ formation is complete.

There have been nine weeks of highly organized cell activity, all controlled and balanced by the underlying genetic code in each cell. Cascades of signals initiate limb development and ensure that liver cells produce plasma proteins rather than fingernails. Errors occur, and it is during these crucial weeks that teratogenic agents such as rubella and other viruses, or drugs (either prescribed or 'recreational') can seriously disrupt the developmental mechanism and give rise to congenital malformation. There is, however, some evidence (for example, the increased incidence of congenital heart defects in monozygotic twins) that pre-implantation events, perhaps cell positioning and relationships, may also be of importance.

During the second trimester (or middle three months) of pregnancy, growth of the fetus is the most obvious sign of development, but these months are very important for brain differentiation. Again cells multiply and migrate in an orderly manner, following established pathways, and any failure to comply has serious consequences for mental development. By 22 - 24 weeks the fetus can be born and starts to have some chance of surviving outside the uterus. Christian attitudes on the very low birthweight infant are fully discussed by Wyatt and Spencer in their recent publication *Survival of the Weakest*[3].

Conclusions

We have traced the stages of fetal development in a superficial manner. Those wishing to go into this fascinating topic in more detail should consult a standard textbook. For those curious to know how messages coded in the DNA can possibly be harnessed to produce the complex patterns of development, Lewis Wolpert's *The Triumph of the Embryo*[1] provides insights into experimental work in various species and gives clues to possible mechanisms.

Embryology is fascinating. Certainly we can see that we are fearfully and wonderfully made, but we have not discovered whether or not the early embryo is a person. At fertilization a unique DNA combination is brought into being, which, if all the necessary support systems come into play, will give rise to a unique person. However, wastage is high, particularly during the pre-implantation stages. Furthermore, most of the cells will develop into the support system, the placenta, and be discarded. Finally there is such totipotency that one fertilized egg may give rise to two people. Biology gives us clues, but does not answer the fundamental question of whether we are dealing with human tissue or a human person. A person must be more than the sum of his or her genes.

We must make a different approach, and turn to Scripture, Church tradition, and the views of philosophers and theologians.

Chapter III
Scriptural and philosophical aspects

This section will start with the early embryo and a historical survey of attitudes towards it. We will then review examples of Roman Catholic and Protestant teaching which illustrate the differing conclusions that have been reached. None provides a conclusive answer. A different approach is to apply the concept of 'value transfer' and view the fetus with the ideal mother's eyes, and this will be explained fully on page 27.

Historical perspective

Many Christians believe that once fertilization has occurred a person is present. This means that the early embryo and later fetus warrant the care due to any human being and abortion would be regarded as murder. It is often claimed that this absolutist view has been the traditional view of the church, and of both early Christians and Old Testament believers.

The writings of Clement of Alexandria, the epistle of Barnabas, and the early Christian manual called *The Didache* can all be quoted as early Christian teaching prohibiting abortion, and therefore implying that the early embryo is sacrosanct. Gordon Dunstan, Professor of Moral Theology, has shown[7] that the concept of absolute protection for the early embryo is a relatively modern one. He believes that the translation of the Hebrew texts into Greek which occurred in the third century BC shows the penalty for abortion to be a graded one, the severity increasing as the pregnancy becomes more advanced. The ancient Hittites adopted this system but the Old Testament verse he refers to (Ex 21:22), which is the only biblical reference to this topic, is a difficult and unsatisfactory one, as the translation of the underlying Hebrew seems uncertain.

Tertullian, an early Christian writer, taught that abortion was homicide from the earliest date of the pregnancy, using the analogy 'just as every fruit is already present in its seed', and a similar view was taken by Basil, Bishop of Caesarea, in the fourth century AD. He specifically used the term 'murder' for the destruction of the fetus, and stressed that there should be no distinction as to whether it was 'formed or unformed'. His brother, Gregory of Nyssa, took a different view, believing that the unformed embryo was not a human being but only a potential one.

The idea of the embryo having a 'formed' and an 'unformed' stage was used by philosophers from the time of Aristotle to try to cope with the dilemma that faces us now. A later fetus looked human and therefore could be accorded human status and protected, but in the early 'blob of cells' stage was it reasonable to give it similar protection? Aristotle, who lived three hundred years before Christ, using the knowledge which was then available stated that as a male fetus was recognisably formed by 40 days it should be considered to be a total human then. The female fetus is less easy to distinguish with certainty, and so 90 days was given as the time of 'humanising' for girls.

This quaint but not unreasonable view held sway over many centuries, and abortion laws were such that penalties for those induced after 'ensoulment' were greater than for those earlier (but both were penalised). This tradition was challenged in 1588 by Pope Sixtus V, who decreed that those who procured an abortion, either early or late, should be considered to be murderers. Even then Christians had firmly held and differing viewpoints, since by 1591 the next Pope rescinded the previous decision, and restored the status quo. The current absolutist view of the Roman Catholic Church stems from a papal bull issued by Pius X in 1869, partly as a remedy for an increasing incidence of abortion at that time. This view is reaffirmed in the *Codex Iuris Canonic* issued in 1983. The reason given for this stance is that if its status is uncertain, then the embryo should be given the benefit of the doubt. This is in general a reasonable viewpoint, but in this particular instance the implications are far-reaching and will be explored more thoroughly in the next chapter.

Roman Catholic writings

The Roman Catholic Church is officially opposed to the use of contraception, believing that with each sexual act the possibility of conception should remain unhindered by artificial means. This Church also teaches that the conception is fully a person from the moment of fertilization, and should therefore be fully protected from then on. Michael Coughlan[8], philosopher from Lampeter, is unconvinced that such legalistic pronouncements truly represent traditional Catholic teaching. He points out that historically declarations based on natural law and reasoned argument could be respected by both believer and unbeliever, whereas current pronouncements depending entirely on Papal authority only have meaning for believers, and so lack universal application.

Dr Teresa Iglesias, a Roman Catholic moral philosopher, has written extensively supporting the absolutist position,[9] arguing strongly that as one's personal history can be traced back to the moment of fertilization this is the time from which each embryo warrants total protection. She stresses the importance of seeing the organism as valuable as a whole, rather than its value being dependent on its various parts, that together make up that whole.

Other examples of Roman Catholic theologians who have made important contributions are John Mahoney, former Principal of Heythrop Theological College, and Norman Ford, Master of the Catholic Theological College in Melbourne, Australia. Neither believes that the time of fertilization is the time at which the status of personhood should be imputed, and their two books are worth reading for their dispassionate attempt to reconcile the traditional Catholic viewpoint with the biological facts. Mahoney[10] points out flaws in discussions based on the idea of the embryo as a 'potential' person, and, at the other extreme, of the proposal that cerebral development should be regarded as crucial. He sees the concept of evolution as helping towards an understanding of the development of a person from human tissue. 'It appears', he says, 'that neither the negative or the positive arguments for immediate ensoulment at conception have probative value, and that the case for a process of organic development leading to the flowering of person-hood is quite an impressively strong one'. Norman Ford's *When did I begin?*[11] traces his search for the answer as he carefully sifted the philosophical, biblical and biological evidence, and includes an exceptionally lucid account of early embryonic development. He started from the classical Roman Catholic position, with fertilization being the crucial point, but finally concluded that the human individual only becomes present with the appearance of the primitive streak, at around day 14 after fertilization.

Biblical teaching on the fetus

Bible teaching about the human fetus is sparse. There are passages describing key individuals such as Jesus or John the Baptist which introduce them at the time of their conception. Isaiah's 'Servant of the Lord', Jeremiah and Paul (Is 49:1,5; Je 1:5; Gal 1:15) all admit to being called by God to their particular task either before or during their time in the womb.

The writer to the Hebrews goes even further, and refers to Levi being in the body of his great-grandfather Abraham (Heb 7:10).

Paul when writing to the Ephesians points out that in fact all Christians were known and called before the creation of the world (Eph 1:4). As God is not con-strained by the dimension of time this is a key concept.

Several passages refer to God's handiwork as he formed the speaker during his time of development (Ps 139; Jb 10:8-12). Psalm 139 is the most dramatic of these passages, as the psalmist clearly looks back at himself while in the womb, indicating a continuity between the present person that he is now, and that which he was then.

What can we learn from this inspired poetry?

The message of the psalm is encapsulated in verse seven:

>Where can I go from your Spirit?
>Where can I flee from your presence?

FACTORS TO BE CONSIDERED AT DIFFERENT STAGES O

	FERTILIZATION	
	Assets	Proble
BIOLOGY	Relatively precise watershed Genetic make-up specified	High (loss r Twinni Embryc suppor system distir Contra methoc a mora
RELATIONSHIPS WITH MOTHER	None	
THEOLOGY/ PHILOSOPHY	Jesus and others named at this stage Origin of 'personal history'	Also to co Only those

	IMPLANTATION Days 10 - 14	LATER 13 - 18 weeks
)	Imprecise Loss rate $\approx$ 15% Primitive streak distinct	Loss rate 2% Resembles a small baby
hable ive omes sue		
	Physically implanted $\downarrow$ awareness of pregnancy	Fetal movements promote bonding
prior ion es to survive	Psalm 139 can well be applied here	

In his imagination, David the psalmist travels north, south, east and west, and affirms that God is present throughout. He tries ascending and descending, but again God is there.

He then takes himself backward in time and follows God's hand moulding him throughout his personal history, right back into his mother's womb. He does not state when his personal history actually starts. Although he does not, and indeed could not, say as much, it would be quite in keeping with the tenor of the writer's thoughts here for him to see God's hand choosing the appropriate egg and sperm with which to initiate him.

This is a psalm extolling God's infinite and all-pervading presence throughout both space and time, and his deep understanding of each individual in every aspect of life.

In the New Testament, Luke, a doctor, takes care to relate the stories of the conception and birth of both John the Baptist and Jesus (Lk 1, 2). In both cases a parent was informed that conception would soon occur and predictions were made about the person to be born, and, most significantly of all, he was given a name. Clearly, therefore, God is aware of the individual from the time of conception and sees a person as a continuum from conception, or probably even from before conception if we look at the genealogies and prophecies concerning the Messiah in the Old Testament (Gen 17:6-7; Is 7:14).

The interpretation of Scripture
The words of Scripture are straightforward but how they should be understood can be more difficult. Christians have interpreted Scriptural teaching in slightly different ways and have reached different conclusions.

The importance of continuity
All conceptions are known by God and their outcome as well. Yet many Christians believe that these passages indicate that he wills all conceptions to develop their full potential. They regard God as seeing the early conceptus as a fully developed person so that we too should accord that conceptus the status of 'neighbour', so discarding the early embryo would therefore be the killing of an innocent person and would always be wrong. Examples of those holding this view include theologians John Stott[12], Oliver O'Donovan[13] and David Atkinson[14]. These authors believe that the undoubted continuity from fertilization to birth makes it clear that 'I am there' from the point of fertilization. John Stott sees this as the crucial message of Psalm 139. He distinguishes the passages dealing with the vocation of the individual being called to his or her task from the time they were in the womb (eg Jeremiah) from our call and election as Christians, which was from before the foundation of the world, (as in Eph 1:4)[12].

The difference of opinion lies in whether or not we believe Psalm 139 to refer to every conception or only to those where the pregnancies continue and give rise to known persons.

God surely knows each fertilized ovum but what we do not know is his purpose for each. Does he will each to develop their full potential or does he know that many are imperfect or destined, for whatever reason, to develop no further? Psalm 139 does not clearly address this question, and without such guidance from Scripture we are left to interpret it in accordance with other aspects of knowledge. Bearing in mind the high natural loss of fertilized ova I find it hard to believe that they are of great importance to God, whereas others take the opposite view, believing all must be precious to him.

Who is my neighbour?
Oliver O'Donovan[13] points out that Jesus, when asked 'who is my neighbour?' (Lk 10:29), did not answer directly, but instead told the story of the Good Samaritan. Likewise, he suggests that our question on the status of the embryo should be answered by working out our attitude to it, rather than by trying to tease out the philosophy. Inevitably, though, how we respond to the embryo will depend on our view of it. It is easier for the non-scientist to imagine him/herself on the Jericho road than in the research laboratory. For the research worker the neighbour who borrows a biro is a thousand times removed from the cluster of cells in the plastic flask.

Who is a parent?
David Atkinson has a different approach[14], with his suggestion that instead of noting when personhood begins, we should ask instead when parenthood begins. From the story of the Annunciation of the birth of Jesus to Mary, in Luke 1, he infers that parenthood starts at the moment of fertilization. The realization of parenthood is, however, for most parents, around the time of the first missed period. A further difficulty with this suggestion is that those using an implantation-preventing mode of contraception would not see themselves, however temporarily, to be parents at all.

He also focuses on the importance of man/woman being made in the image of God. He sees no reason why a very pale image of God should not be present in the earliest embryo. This is a beautiful and even poetic concept, but there does seem to be some confusion of categories between even the palest image of God who is Spirit and the fertilized ovum - a transcript, however complex, of DNA bases.

Scientists' views of the teaching of Scripture

John Medina is a molecular biologist; he agrees with the stance of these theologians, but from an entirely different premise. His book *The Outer Limits of Life*[15] is an excellent, very readable and often humorous description of embryology and early brain development. He candidly portrays his own difficulty in finding the crucial distinction between human tissues and human beings. Despite considerable reservations, he tentatively decides that fusion of egg and sperm must be the instant at which the distinction occurs.

Notwithstanding, he emphasizes that fertilization itself is not as definitive an event as most people suppose. Embryo development can be induced without the aid of sperm and the essential switch mechanism may well be discovered during the next decade, and add a further complication to the debate.

A number of Christians having a high regard for the authority of the Bible as the essential source of our understanding of God and his dealings with us, have reached different conclusions from those outlined above. They find no conflict between Scripture and science, provided Scripture is not expected to answer questions of scientific fact. It is possible to see science and Scripture as complementary, with science answering the 'How?' questions, and Scripture the 'Why?' questions.

One of these is Christian Medical Fellowship member Duncan Vere. In *When is a Person?*[16], he stresses that we must not read into Scripture more than is necessarily there, and he does not believe that the landmark of fertilization need be the crucial point, particularly when we bear in mind the tensions in understanding that arise from God being outside space and time, while we are so limited by these parameters. He sees the early embryo as a 'tent' not yet habitable, which does not yet (in space-time) possess the essential level of development necessary for the expression of a person, for the habitation of that person.

Another is the late Donald Mackay, a physicist[17]. He thought it likely that there was an element of discontinuity in embryonic development. He used the analogy of the smouldering candle suddenly bursting into flame, or the internal combustion engine with the prepared mixture of gases exploding energetically. He thought that at least the development of a nerve network would be a prerequisite of personhood, because brain science indicates that without an adequate endowment of co-operating nerve cells no personal life can come into being. He is, however, careful to stress that he would in no way equate personhood with brain activity.

If not at conception, when might the person begin?

Some suggested biological thresholds
One of the attractions of choosing the moment of fertilization as the crucial time for the person to be fully present is its definiteness. Prior to fusion the egg and the sperm, though each unique, are incapable of giving rise to a healthy individual. Once they have fused, provided all goes well, a baby will be born. Once the crucial time of fusion is rejected as the moment when the person begins, we are left with the dilemma of 'if not then, when?' Biological development continues in a relatively linear manner, and though there are further important thresholds, none is as dramatic as that of fertilization.

Day 14, with the associated phenomena of implantation and primitive streak formation, has been chosen by the Warnock Committee[6] *(see page 33)* as the threshold beyond which embryo research is not allowed. Christians too have suggested thresholds at which the value of the fetus might become absolute. The medieval concept of the formed and unformed fetus has already been discussed *(see page 17)*. In rather different vein, medical student Andrew Thornett takes up the important emphasis on blood as a symbol of life, particularly in the Old Testament[18]. He suggested that the appearance of the fetal blood cells at six weeks could provide a criterion for the presence of life warranting full protection.

The time of 'quickening' at around 16 weeks certainly has an impact on the mother as she feels the baby moving within her, and this has been suggested as a threshold in the past.

Others, for example Gardner[5], believe that taking the first breath is the crucial step. As Genesis 2:7 describes God making man by 'breathing the breath of life' into Adam, this important threshold does have some attractions, but is probably untenable today as premature babies can now be ventilated for several weeks before they breathe spontaneously.

A biological or a spiritual threshold?
A search for biological thresholds seems inherently unsatisfactory, because our personhood is not biologically determined. God is Spirit and his image in us, our distinctiveness as individual people, may be expressed by our bodies, but is more than physical. The essential 'me' or 'you' is a 'spiritual' or intangible being who leaves the body at death. We will therefore approach the question from a different aspect. We will consider humankind, and how their being made in the image of God makes them distinct from the animals, and see whether the concept of value transfer can help us understand the value of the embryo.

Made in the image of God?

The story of the creation in Genesis 1 describes how God made the plants, the animals, and finally the man and the woman. We have seen that we share our DNA with the plant and animal kingdom. God made humans a special creation in his own image.

Genesis 1:27 states: 'So God created man in his own image, in the image of God he created him; male and female he created them'.

The image of God is not a DNA sequence, the specific DNA sequence is a vehicle for the image of God in that particular person. Human beings have a set of human genes, but that is not the essence of their humanity.

What then is the 'image of God' which makes humankind different from the animals? Philosophers and theologians still grapple with this concept. All that can be done here is to offer some of their words as they struggle to express the inexpressible.

Brunner (1939)[19]

> Man's meaning and his intrinsic worth do not reside in himself, but in the One who stands 'over against' him ... Man's distinctiveness is not based upon the power of his muscles or the acuteness of his sense organs, but upon the fact that he participates in the life of God ...

Anderson (1982)[20]

> What is unique and distinctive to human beings is not an absolute physical, or even psychical differentiation between humans and animal creatures. The distinction must be found elsewhere ... Non-human creatures do not participate in the fellowship and relation with God designated by the Seventh Day ... The human may be differentiated from all that is of the Sixth Day, even its own creaturely nature, by the Creator's summons to participate in the Seventh Day.

He believes that we can gain some understanding of what is meant by our capacity to relate to God by looking at Adam's response and recognition of Eve as a 'soulmate'. He goes on to develop the idea further with emphasis on man's use of the Sabbath rest for recreation through worship and relationship with God. He believes that the 'image' or reflection of God presupposes 'encounter' with God and that it is this encounter with God which is the essence of being human.

Another theologian expresses the same concepts in a different way; man is distinctive in that he alone is 'faced by God and has to make responsible decisions before Him' (Barth)[21]. This is an area of mystery and depth. There is no glib answer to the question 'What is man?' The psalmist answers 'You made him a little lower than God (or 'the angels', in some translations), and crowned him with glory and honour' (Ps 8:4-5). If God gives his human creatures such honour we can but follow his example.

The concept of 'value transfer'

John Medina[15] suggests that this is a form of 'value transfer'. By this he means the increase in value or change in status that occurs when some respected authority bestows value on an object. The stock market may be influenced by the purchases of a few major dealers, a school will have a special status once Royalty has sent its child there!

Earlier in his book he tells the story of the senior scientist who in casual conversation made it clear that if a choice had to be made, he would save the life of his beloved cat in preference to that of an unknown child. This he said was because he had a real relationship with his cat, and none with the child. This illustrates the hazard of attaching total importance to relationships, but also makes one ask the question 'Why are we shocked (*are* we shocked?) that the cat is given preference to the child?'

Some, such as Australian philosopher Peter Singer[22], believe such a view to be species-ist, and maintain that animals and humans should be equally respected. As Christians we could not agree. At the lowest level this could simply be in obedience to the command to love our neighbour as ourself. But surely there is much more to it than that.

Christians know that God has demonstrated the particular value he places on people because it is only they that have been created in his own image, and, even more striking, it is for humans that Christ died. Jesus's teaching focuses on people and their worth, adults and children, well and sick, rich and poor. Peter on the day of Pentecost (Acts 2:39) tells those who enquire that the promise is to them and to their children. This is the reason for our care and it is here that we find the reason for our concern about the status of the embryo. Either it is human tissue, valuable in its own right but not yet a human person, or it is my brother for whom Christ died, my neighbour whom I must love as myself.

Who values the embryo?

Can we use the concept of 'value transfer' to help us discover the value of the embryo? We know we have responsibility as our brother's (or sister's) keeper. Does God's design suggest that he has delegated to the mother the role of 'embryo keeper'? We have seen earlier (*page 11*) that the mother is entirely unaware of the moment or process of fertilization. She may pass fertilized or unfertilized ova out of her body, and which passes may depend upon the method of contraception she uses.

Once implanted, the embryo signals its presence to the mother, and all her biological instincts come into play to make her behave very much as the embryo's keeper. She usually recognises herself to be pregnant and in the normal course of events feels very protective towards the developing embryo. She may alter her diet or lifestyle, and is upset if any untoward event such as bleeding occurs. The embryo certainly has value to her now. We may reasonably try to extrapolate from the natural order of God's creation, and perhaps we find here a clue to God's attitude to the very early embryo. Biologically he has delegated its care to the mother, but it is only after implantation that her nurturing role comes into action. Can we follow this lead and accept that prior to implantation it may not be a valued human person?

Exceptions to consider

There are of course times when the pre-implantation embryo, or even individual ova, are of value to the mother. If she is in the process of an *in vitro* fertilization procedure, where ova recently retrieved, and either fertilized or not, were inadvertently discarded or dropped on the floor, this would be a real loss, but this would be chiefly because of the effort invested in them.

Alternatively, we know that it is possible for the mother to fail to value her fetus, and to request abortion, but this is a separate and major issue which cannot be tackled here. The point to be made is *not* that the value of the fetus is dependent on its mother's attitude to it. This would be patently illogical and wrong. The point is that in his wisdom God seems to have arranged the natural order so that the mother only becomes aware of her fetus and able to value it *after* implantation has taken place. Is there any suggestion here that God himself values the embryo more after implantation?

Medical practice and attitudes to the fetus

We respect the developing fetus partly because of its value to its mother, who is our neighbour. When abortion is done after a chorion biopsy has shown the fetus to be affected with, for example, severe muscular dystrophy, there is sadness in the medical staff involved. They are sad not chiefly for the fetus who will not be born, but mainly for the parents whose hopes are disappointed, and who have decided to end a wanted pregnancy. A somewhat similar attitude is seen in Scripture, when Matthew describes the Slaughter of the Innocents. He quotes the verse describing Rachel weeping for her children (Mt 2:18) rather than focusing on the loss of infant life.

Thus our treating of the parents, in particular the mother, as our neighbour involves us in sharing her valuing of the post-implantation embryo, and later fetus.

Conclusions

In summary, therefore, Scripture does not give as clearcut teaching as many assume on how we should value the very early embryo. Biology shows the pre-implantation embryo to have the potential to travel down a number of different developmental pathways. Only a small part of it is destined to become the embryo itself, and there is a high wastage rate of whole embryos, all giving an impression of imprecision and prodigality. The loss of these early pre-implantation embryos, whose presence remains unknown to anybody, can in no way be compared with the loss of beloved children through famine, or even with loss through miscarriage. Both of these have an impact on parents.

At implantation the embryo establishes a relationship with the mother and (ideally) becomes valued by her. Perhaps we can take up this clue, and like the mother afford the embryo no essential value prior to implantation. After this, with increasing growth and development, its status increases for both mother and her attendants. But when is the image of God fully present? When is this my neighbour for whom Christ died? Is this a gradual process or a decisive moment? Or are we asking the wrong questions?

Chapter IV
Practical applications

Does it matter what we believe about the value of the embryo? If we do not clearly understand its status, should we not be on the safe side and give the pre-implantation embryo the benefit of the doubt? This may seem a very reasonable viewpoint, but we need to take care that this is not an excuse for failing to face the issues or a selfish concern to keep our own hands clean. Where does our view of the embryo impinge on everyday life? The four most important areas are contraception, in vitro fertilization, pre-implantation diagnosis and embryo experimentation. Although the second and third of these may only involve a few, the majority of adults have to make decisions about the first.

Why do we exist?
However, before going on to these practical issues, we need to consider the somewhat mind-stretching matter of what Gareth Jones, Professor of Anatomy in Dunedin, calls *non-existence*[23]. He describes a couple initially with two children, who later decided to have two more. These two later children might well not have existed, and only came into being because their parents changed their minds. Parents can choose to bring or not to bring children into the world, and to act as co-creators with God. We agonize over the morality of artificial reproduction, but seldom stand back and review the awe-ful decisions we make, or fail to make, when children are conceived in the standard way.

Gareth Jones goes on to explore as a Christian the different modes by which the non-existence of the two children might have been accomplished: by abstinence, or by various forms of contraception including the prevention of implantation of the fertilized ovum. He cannot see any moral difference, the end result being that the children do not exist, and the parents are totally unaware as to whether or not fertilization ever actually occurred. For them the crucial decision is whether or not they will bring another person into the world, and it is this decision that involves them. When conception occurs, and develops into a recognized pregnancy, the situation is different. Decisions about abortion do have an impact on the parents, so that although the child is never known, it has some effect on the parents' lives. He concludes that we are finding the area of reproductive technology so difficult because of 'our lack of analysis of the nature of our day-to-day decision-making in the reproductive area, the result being that we are unprepared for the very precise decision-making now being demanded of us'.

This is a challenge we all need to take seriously.

Four practical procedures

1. Contraception

It is in our decisions about contraception that the majority of parents 'act God'. Once we accept contraception as legitimate for Christians, a responsible form of stewardship enabling us to maintain the marriage relationship and yet not over-burden either ourselves or the planet, we have made a far-reaching decision. Not only does contraception separate the procreative and relationship aspects of sexual intercourse, but it also empowers us to bring certain people into the world, but to keep others out. Those of us who make use of contraception continue to see children as gifts from God but believe that he has enabled us to make responsible choices as to their number.

Contraception's mode of action

Several forms of contraception are thought to act by preventing implantation of the fertilized ovum. The intra-uterine device is the most widely recognised of these, but the mechanisms of action of the progestagen-only oral contraceptive pills are not fully understood.

Certainly large doses of oestrogen taken as a 'morning after' pill act to prevent implantation rather than fertilization. This can either be seen as a measure of pre-vention or as an abortifacient, depending on one's views on the status of the pre-implantation embryo. There are two separate moral issues here: we must consider not only the mode of action of the medication but also, and probably more impor-tantly, the reason it is needed. Rape is the most violent and obvious breach of God's laws, but the one-night-stand or spur-of-the-moment adultery are also offensive in God's eyes. By comparison, the need for such a pill could arise following a split sheath for a couple at high risk of fetal abnormality, who were avoiding pregnancy because they would not contemplate abortion. In general, therefore, we need to weigh up the reason for contraceptive use as carefully as the means by which it is to be achieved, and in my personal view it is the former which should be the chief focus of attention.

The only further point to be made is that the need for reliable contraception is one of the world's most pressing current material problems, and such decisions affect the majority of any adult population at some stage in their lives.

2. In vitro fertilization

Louise Brown, the first test-tube baby, was born in 1978, and so is now a teenager. A recent photograph in a national newspaper showed the girl who was the first 'test-tube baby' from one centre, cradling their newly-born thousandth. The number of such children in the world continues to increase, but it must be remembered that for every pair of delighted parents, there are likely to be one or two who are further depressed by failing in yet another attempt to have a family.

In vitro fertilization involves fusion of ovum and sperm in the laboratory, followed by a few days' culture of the multiplying cells, with the embryo then being returned to the mother's uterus. In order to increase the success rate, it has been essential to try different methods, and culture routines, and inevitably this results in many embryos being discarded. Improved methods do however now mean that the success rate per cycle in good centres is approaching that of natural fertilization[24]. Although a couple may opt to keep all their own fertilized ova, it has to be accepted that discarding of fertilized ova has been inherent in the development of these techniques, so that those who see this as tantamount to murder should avoid all aspects of in vitro fertilization.

Couples who do decide to proceed with this technique may be faced with the problem of what to do with the 'spare' embryos. Usually a number of ova are fertilized to be sure that there are enough healthy embryos to return to the uterus. In the early days, to try to maximise success, four or five might be returned, and multiple pregnancies occurred frequently. Now only two or perhaps three embryos are used, and there may well be some left over. These can either be discarded, or frozen so that the couple can make use of them should the current attempt fail, or be used for research (*see page 35*).

Putting aside the matter of embryo disposal, the principle of in vitro fertilization with the use of gametes from husband and wife seems morally reasonably straightforward, and many Christians have decided before God to have a baby this way. The possibility of in vitro fertilization does, however, make technically possible a whole host of other scenarios: donation of sperm, ova or embryos, giving rise to children whose genetic parents are quite distinct from their rearing parents. These are major moral dilemmas, but as they do not relate directly to the status of the embryo, they will not be considered further here. Those wishing to go further on this topic should read Gareth Jones's book, *Manufacturing Humans*[25]. He reviews all the ramifications from a Christian standpoint, and concludes with a set of guidelines for society as a whole, and some practical advice for the Christian couple considering use of this technique.

The Human Fertilization and Embryology Act 1990

It was the possibility of such developments, as well as concern about the nature of the embryo, that prompted the Government to set up a Committee of Enquiry under the leadership of Mary (now Baroness) Warnock[6]. Their report was published in 1984, but it was not until 1990 that the Human Fertilization and

Embryology Bill passed through Parliament. It covers all aspects of in vitro fertilization and related reproductive techniques, and makes specific stipulations about the embryo itself.

The Law permits research on the human embryo for 14 days after fertilization, or until the appearance of the primitive streak (whichever is the sooner). Research can only be undertaken in licensed premises, and must be the responsibility of an established research worker, whose credentials are taken into account during the licensing procedure. No embryo that has been the subject of an experiment may be returned to the uterus, and certain types of research are banned. For a detailed account of the law and its implications, see *Blackstone's Guide to the Act*[26].

A clause in the 1990 Bill set the limit for the majority of terminations of pregnancy at 24 weeks gestation, but permitted termination on grounds of severe fetal handicap at any gestational age. Many Christians see a glaring anachronism here, with the 15-day embryo having the protection of the law, and the fetus having none. However, the embryo to which the law refers is isolated, and motherless, and is being protected from the research worker.

3. Pre-implantation diagnosis

Many couples who are at high risk of having a child with a serious genetic disorder decide to use prenatal diagnosis and abortion in order to avoid the birth of an affected child. The mother becomes pregnant, and at about 10 weeks into the pregnancy a chorion biopsy is taken, and the necessary laboratory tests are done on this tissue. The result should be available in two or three weeks, and parents are either overjoyed, or faced with the misery of aborting a longed-for pregnancy. Many couples find this more than they can cope with, particularly if two successive pregnancies are affected. Others find abortion totally unacceptable, and therefore do not make use of such an approach.

It has recently become possible to perform the diagnostic tests on just one or two cells, and this has opened the door to what is called *pre-implantation diagnosis*. The ovum is fertilized using standard in vitro techniques, and the early cell divisions allowed to occur. After three days, when about eight cells are present, it is possible to remove one cell, and test for the presence or absence of the harmful gene. If it is present, the pre-implantation embryo will be discarded, and only healthy ones returned to the uterus. Pregnancy can then continue unhindered, in the normal way.

So far it is technically only possible to tell the sex of the fetus, and to diagnose cystic fibrosis. It is still very early days, but provided the technique is shown to be safe then testing for other diseases will become possible, and many couples will be spared the trauma of becoming pregnant knowing that abortion is a real possibility in six to eight weeks' time. The number of babies born using this technique is still very small, as at the time of writing five have been born and two are in the later stages of pregnancy, and there has been one miscarriage[27]. These pregnancies have all been tested at one centre, and 26 couples participated. The success rate is therefore still low, but the children who have been born appear entirely normal. It could be argued that it is wrong for parents to make use of a technique which, although shown to be safe on animals, is relatively unproven in humans. Yet such is the desire of parents to avoid abortion that the centres doing this highly specialised work have large numbers of couples wanting to participate.

4. Embryo research

In order to develop tests so that the technique can be applied to an increasing number of disorders, research has to be done on pre-implantation embryos. It would be wrong to use such a technique clinically until the workers were confident that they could give a reliable result to the couple requesting the test. Thus work on embryos which will be discarded is inherent in the development of any of the techniques described. This type of research is very clearly applied to solving specific clinical problems.

There are many other avenues which can be explored by studying the fertilized egg and developing embryo. The mechanisms of fertilization itself are becoming better understood, and new methods of contraception may well be developed. The fact that the genes inherited from each parent seem to have different roles during embryogenesis is an unexpected finding with practical application to our understanding of the causes of congenital malformations. The whole concept of the switch from a cell with multiple potentials to one committed to become embryo or embryonic membrane is another area full of promise for providing new insights not only into embryology, but also into the mechanisms of malignant (cancerous) change.

It is too early to know what benefits will accrue from this research, but at present we have to admit that we are woefully ignorant about the causes of errors in embryo development, and this is reflected in the number of babies born with congenital malformations, the rate of which has altered little since the start of the century.

Another aspect of embryo research that needs consideration is the matter of *how should embryos be obtained?*

In the early days of in vitro fertilization, couples might well have spare embryos which they were prepared to donate for research. Now that embryos can be frozen, there are fewer spare embryos available, and we are faced with the concept that embryos may be created specifically to be used for research, and then discarded. In the original Warnock Committee this issue gave rise to a minority report as three members were unable to accept embryo research at all, and four thought it wrong to create embryos for this purpose. Gordon Dunstan, Professor of Moral Theology, believes the distinction to be a false one, and argues that if research is to be done, it is better to use 'donated' rather than spare embryos since their supply is less haphazard.

Some Christians, such as Professor David Short[28], have in the past called for a moratorium on all embryo research, partly because of concern for the embryo, but also because research could be misused, and open up a veritable Pandora's Box. There are certainly aspects of embryo research which, quite apart from the status of the embryo, should give Christians cause for concern. If we can identify disease genes, we might one day be able to identify genes for normal traits such as height or hair colour, or perhaps athletic ability. Should parents be able to avail themselves of such choices? Will we start to see children as consumer products rather than as God's gifts?[29]

Conclusion

This brief outline gives some idea as to the scope of embryo manipulation. It emphasises the importance of reaching the right conclusions on the nature of the embryo. Either a Christian should advocate the banning of all such research, or we see here a new and exciting field in which to explore God's handiwork. For those of us who accept the latter view there is the challenge to ensure that there are guidelines, and regulations for responsible research. If research is to be done, Christians need to be involved, and to make their contribution towards it being done wisely and well.

References

[1] Wolpert L, *The Triumph of the Embryo.* Oxford University Press, Oxford. 1991.

[2] Tooley M, *Abortion and Infanticide.* Oxford University Press, Oxford. 1984.

[3] Wyatt J S and Spencer A, *Survival of the Weakest.* CMF, London. 1992.

[4] Stirrat G M, L*egalised Abortion - the Continuing Dilemma.* CMF, London. 1979.

[5] Gardner R F R, *Abortion. The Personal Dilemma.* Paternoster, Exeter. 1972.

[6] R*eport of the Committee of Enquiry into Human Fertilisation and Embryology* (Warnock Committee). Her Majesty's Stationery Office, London. 1984.

[7] Dunstan G R, 'The moral status of the human embryo: a tradition recalled?' *J Medical Ethics,* 1984; **10:** 38-44.

[8] Coughlan M J, *The Vatican, the Law and the Human Embryo.* Macmillan, London. 1990.

[9] Iglesias T, 'What kind of being is the human embryo?' In *Embryos and Ethics* (ed Cameron N M de S). Rutherford House, Edinburgh. 1987.

[10] Mahoney J, *Bioethics and Belief.* Sheed and Ward, London. 1984.

[11] Ford N M, *When did I begin?* Cambridge University Press, Cambridge. 1988.

[12] Stott J R W, *Issues Facing Christians Today.* Marshall Morgan and Scott, Basingstoke. 1984. Chapter 15.

[13] O'Donovan O, *Begotten or Made?* Oxford University Press, Oxford. 1984. p60.

[14] Atkinson D, 'Some theological perspectives on the human embryo.' In *Embryos and Ethics* (ed. Cameron N M de S). Rutherford House, Edinburgh. 1987.

[15] Medina J, *The Outer Limits of Life.* Nelson, Nashville. 1991.

[16] Vere D W, 'When is a person?' *Journal of the Christian Medical Fellowship,* 1988; **34:** 18-23.

[17] Mackay D, 'The beginnings of personal life.' *In The Service of Medicine,* 1984; **30:** 9-13.

[18] Thornett A, 'Abortion - an emotive issue.' *Nucleus,* 1992; **April:** 20-23.

[19] Brunner H E, *Man in Revolt.* Lutterworth, Cambridge. 1939.

[20] Anderson R S, *On Being Human.* William B Eardmans, Michigan. 1982. p23.

[21] Barth K, *Church Dogmatics.* T and T Clark, Edinburgh. 1961.

[22] Singer P, *Animal Liberation.* Cape, London. 1976.

[23] Jones D G, 'Non-existence and its relevance for Medical Ethics and Genetic Technology.' *Perspectives on Science and Christian Faith,* 1991; **43:** 75-81.

[24] Hull M G R, Eddowes H A, Fahy U U, Abuzed M I, Mills M S, Cahill D J, Fleming C F, Wardle P G, Ford W C L and McDermott A. *Expectations of assisted conception for infertility.* Br Med J, 1992; **304:** 1465-1469.

[25] Jones D G, *Manufacturing humans.* IVP, Leicester. 1987.

[26] Morgan D and Lee R G, *Blackstone's Guide to the Human Fertilization and Embryology Act, 1990.* Blackstone, London. 1991.

[27] Winston R, *Preimplantation Diagnosis.* Carter Memorial Lecture, British Medical Genetics Conference, Nottingham. 1992.

[28] Short D S, 'Embryo experimentation: the case for a moratorium.' *In The Service of Medicine,* 1985; **31:** 2-3.

[29] CMF Specialist Committee on Genetics. 'Submission to the British Medical Association Working Party on Genetic Engineering.' *Journal of the Christian Medical Fellowship,* 1990; **36:** 18-22.

Glossary of Technical Terms

Words in italics occur in the glossary in their own right

Abortifacient	Any agent which will induce an established pregnancy to abort.
Amino Acid	An organic acid from which proteins are built. There are 20 amino acids essential to life and each is specified by its own triplet of *bases.* eg Amino acid serine is produced by bases TCG while GCT will give rise to amino acid alanine.
Amino Acid Synthesis	Process by which *amino acids* are made from simpler chemicals present in the cell.
Base	A molecule containing carbon, nitrogen, hydrogen and oxygen which goes to make up the *DNA.* The four essential bases are: adenine (A) thymine (T) guanine (G) and cytosine (C).
Chorion Biopsy	or *Chorion Villus Sampling.* A technique whereby a tiny piece of the developing placenta can be obtained when the pregnancy is about 10 weeks old (8 weeks after fertilization). Results of tests on this tissue can give information about the developing embryo.

Chromosome	A thread-like body of *DNA* in the cell *nucleus* which can be seen under the microscope when the cell divides. In humans the *DNA* is packaged into the 23 pairs of chromosomes.
Cystic Fibrosis	A genetically determined disease affecting the lungs and digestive system.
Cytoplasm	The part of the cell that is not the nucleus.
DNA	Abbreviation for deoxyribonucleic acid. It is a long, thin chain-like molecule, usually occuring as two complementary chains and made up of thousands of *bases*. The precise arrangement of these four bases, repeated many times, is used to store all the information necessary for life.
Embryo	Term applied to the developing human (or animal) from fertilization until the organs are formed. In humans usually used for the first 12 weeks after which the term *fetus* is often used.
Embryogenesis	The development of the *embryo* from fertilization onwards.
Enzyme	A protein molecule whose function is to catalyze (accelerate) a biological chemical reaction.
Fetus	The developing baby while in the womb. The term *embryo* is commonly used during the earlier stages of development.
Gamete	Term used to denote either egg or sperm cell. (See also *Germ Cells.*)
Gene	A small section of *DNA* that contains information for construction of one protein molecule or part thereof.
Genetic Code	The concept that each *amino acid* is specifically represented by its own triplet of *bases.* eg Triplet TCG gives rise to the *amino acid* serine while GCT gives rise to *amino acid* alanine.
Genome	The entire genetic make up.
Germ Cells	The egg or the sperm or their precursor cells. Each has only one set of *chromosomes.*
Hydatidiform Mole	A conception consisting of placental tissue but no embryo. It may be *triploid* or if the *chromosome* number is correct both sets of chromosomes may be derived from the father.
Intron	A sequence of *DNA* which may be thousands of *bases* long which does not appear to contribute any useful information. Sometimes referred to as 'junk *DNA*'.

Meiosis	The two cell divisions whereby the *germ cells* are produced having (in humans) only 23 *chromosomes* instead of the usual 23 pairs (46) found in the other cells of the body.
Mitochondria	Structures found in the *cytoplasm* of the cell which have their own *DNA* system.
Notochord	A solid rod of cells which appears early in the development of the *embryo* proper.
Nucleus	A distinct part of the cell which contains the *chromosomes*.
Oestrogen	Female hormone.
Primitive Streak	A piling up of cells at one end of the embryonic disc which provides the earliest evidence of the formation of the actual *embryo* itself.
Progestagen	Female hormone concerned with preparing the uterus (womb) for pregnancy.
Sequence	When applied to *DNA* indicates the order of the bases in that particular stretch of *DNA*.
Teratogen	An agent which can damage the developing *embryo* (eg the rubella - german measles - virus).
Totipotent	Having the capacity to develop into any part of the *embryo* or its support system.
Triploid	Having three sets of *chromosomes* instead of the usual pairs. A human *embryo* with 69 instead of 46 chromosomes cannot survive long term.
Zygote	The fertilized egg before it undergoes any further development.

BLOODAXE PAMP

Fleur Adcock

MEETING THE COMET

BLOODAXE BOOKS

ISBN: 1 85224 053 9 limited signed hardback edition
       1 85224 054 7 ordinary edition

First published 1988 by
Bloodaxe Books Ltd,
P.O. Box 1SN,
Newcastle upon Tyne NE99 1SN.

Bloodaxe Books Ltd acknowledges
the financial assistance of Northern Arts.

Typesetting by Bryan Williamson, Manchester.

Limited signed hardback edition
bound by DJB Book Binders, Newcastle upon Tyne.

Ordinary edition bound by
John Joyce & Son, Gateshead, Tyne and Wear.

Printed in Great Britain by
Tyneside Free Press Workshop Ltd, Newcastle upon Tyne.

BEFORE

1

She'll never be able to play the piano –
well, not properly. She'll never be able
to play the recorder, even, at school,
when she goes: it has so many little holes . . .

We'll have her taught the violin.
Lucky her left hand's the one with four
fingers, one for each string. A thumb
and a fleshy fork are enough to hold a bow.

2

Before the calculator – the electronic one –
there were beads to count on; there was the abacus
to tell a tally or compute a score;
or there were your fingers, if you had enough.

The base was decimal: there had to be
a total of ten digits, in two sets –
a bunch of five, another bunch of five.
If they didn't match, your computations went haywire.

3

On the left hand, four and a thumb.
On the right, a thumb and just two.
Proper fingers, true, fitted out
in the standard way; but not four.

Baby-plump, the wrist on the left.
On the right, the arm narrows down
to a slender stem and a palm
like a little tube of soft bones.

4

Leafy lanes and *rus in urbe* were the thing
for a sheltered childhood (not that it was for long,
but parents try): the elm trees lingering
behind the coach-factory; the tense monotonous song

of collared doves; the acres of bare floor
for learning to gallop on in the first size
of Start-Rite shoes; the peacock glass in the front door;
and the swift refocusing lurch of the new baby-sitter's eyes.

5

The Duke of Edinburgh stance: how cute
in a five-year-old! She doesn't do it much
when you're behind her; then it's hands in armpits
or pockets. School, of course, would like to teach

that well-adjusted children don't need pockets
except for their normal purposes, to hold
hankies or bus-tickets. She'll not quite learn
what she's not quite specifically told.

6

Perhaps I don't exist. Perhaps
I didn't exist till I thought that;
then God invented me and made me
the age I am now (nearly eight);

perhaps I was someone else before,
and he suddenly swapped us round, and said
'You can be the girl with two fingers
and she can be you for a change, instead.'

7

'Give us your hand – it's a bit muddy here,
you'll slip.' But he's on her wrong side: her right's
wrong. She tries to circumnavigate him
('Watch it!' he says), to offer him her left –

and slips. It comes out. 'There!' she says. 'You see!'
'Is that all? Fucking hell,' he says, 'that's nothing;
don't worry about it, love. My Auntie May
lost a whole arm in a crash. Is it hereditary?'

8

'Some tiny bud that should have split into four
didn't, we don't know why' was all they could offer.
Research, as usual, lags. But suddenly, this:
'A long-term study has found a positive link

between birth defects and exposure to pesticides
in the first twelve weeks of pregnancy . . . the baby's
neural crest . . . mothers who had been present when
aerosol insecticides . . .' Now they tell us.

TRAVELLING

9 *So far*

She has not got multiple sclerosis.
She has not got motorneuron disease,
or muscular dystrophy, or Down's Syndrome,
or a cleft palate, or a hole in the heart.

Her sight and hearing seem to be sound.
She has not been damaged by malnutrition,
or tuberculosis, or diabetes.
She has not got (probably not got) cancer.

10 *Passport*

Date of birth and all that stuff: straightforward;
likewise, now that she's stopped growing, height.
But ah, 'Distinguishing marks': how can she smuggle
so glaring a distinction out of sight?

The Passport Office proves, in one of its human
incarnations, capable of tact:
a form of words emerges that fades down
her rare statistic to a lustreless fact.

11 *Stars*

She's seeing stars – Orion steady on her left
like a lit-up kite (she has a window-seat)
and her whole small frame of sky strung out
with Christmas-tree lights. But what's all that

behind them? Spilt sugar? Spangled faults
in the plane's window? A dust of glittering points
like the sparkle-stuff her mother wouldn't let her
wear on her eyes to the third-form party.

12 *Halfway*

Does less mean more? She's felt more nearly naked
in duffel-coat and boots and scarf
with nothing showing but a face and her bare
fingers (except, of course, for the times

in fur gloves – mittens – look, no hands!)
than here on a beach in a bikini:
flesh all over. Look at my legs, my
back, my front. Shall I take off my top?

13 *At the airport*

Shoulders like horses' bums; an upper arm
dressed in a wobbling watermelon of flesh
and a frilly muu-muu sleeve; red puckered necks
above the bougainvillaea and sunsets

and straining buttons of Hawaiian shirts;
bellies; bald heads; a wilting grey moustache
beneath a hat proclaiming 'One Old Poop'.
The tour guide rounds them up: his travelling freak-show.

14   *Comet*

'There will be twenty telescopes in the crater
of Mount Albert.' White-coated figures man them,
marshalling queues in darkness: not the Klan
but the Lions raising funds for charity.

$2 a look. No lights – not even torches;
no smoking (bad for the optics); no moon
above the tree-fringed walls of this grassy dip.
Nothing up there but stars. And it, of course.

15 *Halley party*

A glow-worm in a Marmite jar
like the one her mother brought her once:
'I dreamt you woke me in the night and showed me
a glow-worm in a Marmite jar.'

So these wee kids in dressing-gowns
will remember being woken up
for honey sandwiches and cocoa
and a little light in a ring of glass.

16 *Orbit*

'It's not like anything else, with its stumpy tail:
just a fuzz, really, until you get up close –
but of course you can't. With binoculars, I meant,
or a telescope. Actually the tail's fading.'

Higher than Scorpius now, higher than the Pointers,
high as the mid-heaven, she's tracked it nightly,
changing. 'I'm not the only one, but I'm once
in a lifetime.' As for close, that's something else.

AFTER

17

Landing at Gatwick on a grey Sunday when
the baggage handlers seem to be on strike as
they were at the airport before last (but no,
it's merely Britain being its old self) she's

her old self – a self consisting also of
more hand-luggage than she'd thought she was allowed
plus her at last reclaimed suitcase: all of which,
however she may dispose them, hurt her hand.

18

Rise above it! Swallow a chemical:
chuck down whisky, Valium, speed,
Mogadon, caffeine; bomb it or drown it.
But wait! If chemicals did the deed

pandering to their ways compounds
the offence. Resist: you know they lead
to trouble. Find another obsession.
Face a healthier form of need.

19

Saving the world is the only valid cause.
Now that she knows it's round it seems smaller,
more vulnerable (as well as bigger, looser,
a baggy bundle of dangerous contradictions).

There's room for such concerns in student life,
if you stretch it. So: Link hands around the world
for peace! Thumbs down to Star Wars! Hands off
the environment! Two fingers to the Bomb!

20

'Of course you'd have a natural sympathy . . .
I always thought it was quite sweet, your little hand,
when we were kids; but we don't want other kids
walking around the world with worse things . . .

I'm not upsetting you, am I?' No, she's not,
this warm voice from the past, this candid face.
'Right. See you tomorrow. The coach leaves at 8.
Oh, and we've got a wonderful furious banner.'

21

The fountain in her heart informs her
she needn't try to sleep tonight –
rush, gush: the sleep-extinguisher
frothing in her chest like a dishwasher.

She sits at the window with a blanket
to track the turning stars. A comet
might add some point. The moon ignores her;
but dawn may come. She'd settle for that.

22

There was a young woman who fell
for someone she knew rather well –
a friend from her school: confirming the rule
that with these things you never can tell.

The person she'd thought a fixed star –
stuck on rails like a tram, not a car –
shot off into orbit and seemed a new planet,
and a dazzler, the finest by far.

23

She wants to see what it looks like on
a breast. She puts it on a breast –
not the one she has in mind
but her own: at least it's a rehearsal.

Three weeks later, the first night:
a nipple, darker than hers, framed
in a silky, jointed bifurcation.
There is also dialogue. And applause.

24

And she never did learn to play the violin.
So it will have to be *Musica Mundana*,
"the harmony of the spheres" (coming across a map
of the southern skies cut out of some Auckland paper)

or the other kind: what was it? *Instrumentalis*
and – ah, yes – *Humana*. (Listen: Canopus, Crux,
Carina, Libra, Vela choiring together. She
has glided right off the edge of the star-chart.)